Count With Me In FULA

·····By Haby Bah·····

ISBN: 978-1-78324-288-7

Book design by Wordzworth
www.wordzworth.com

1

2 3

4 5 6

7 8 9 10

Go'o

(Goh'oh)

1

One

Didi

(Dhidhi)

Two

Tati

(Tahti)

Three

Nay

(Nahyi)

Four

Jowi

(Joewi)

5

Five

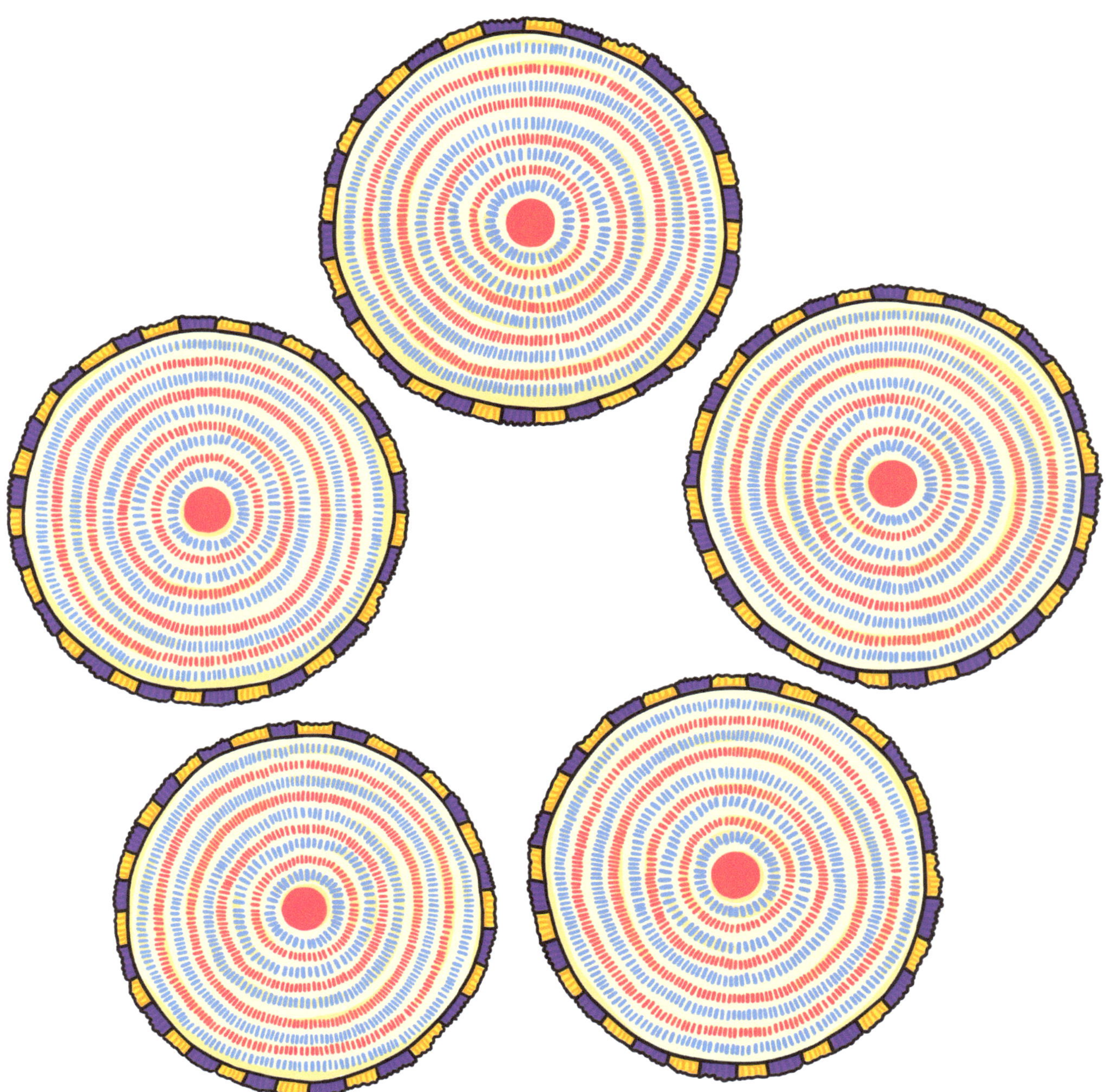

Jeego

(Jehgoh)

6

Six

Jeedhi

(Jehdhidhi)

Seven

Jeetati

(Jehtati)

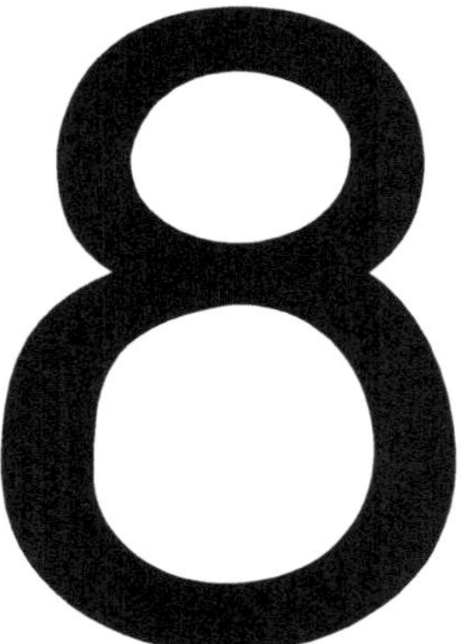

Eight

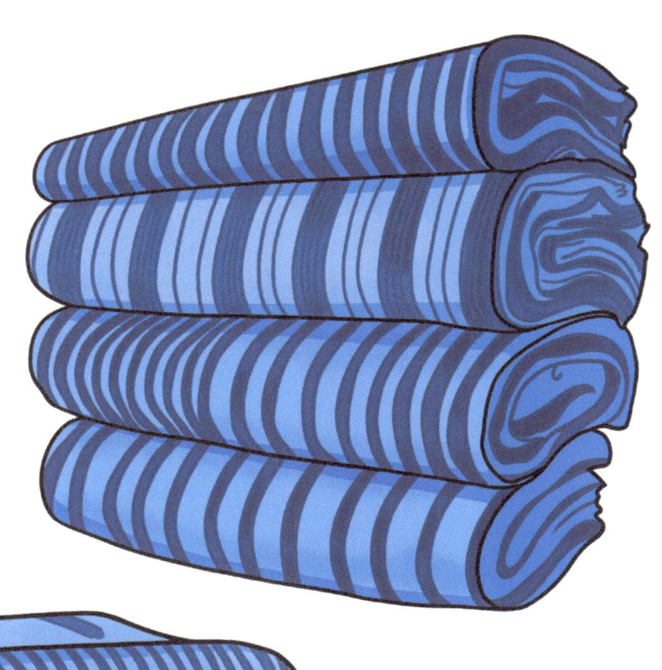

Jeenay

(Jeenayi)

9

Nine

Sappo

(Sappoh)

10

Ten

www.ingramcontent.com/pod-product-compliance
Lightning Source LLC
LaVergne TN
LVHW071630100826
845154LV00007BA/118
9781783242887